Esther the Eaglet

A True Story of Rescue and Rehabilitation

by Christie Gove-Berg

Adventure Publications, Inc.
Cambridge, MN

To Mary and Peter Gove, for their love and support; I could not ask for better parents.

Acknowledgements

Thank you to my husband Pete and our kids, Owen, Adelyn and Annamarie, for cheering me on; to Gail Buhl and The Raptor Center at the University of Minnesota for the photographs, knowledge, enthusiasm and mission to protect and rehabilitate injured raptors; to Holly Harden, my friend and teacher; and to the talented and generous photographers who donated their work so that this story could be told in photos: Gail Buhl and The Raptor Center at the University of Minnesota, Glenn and Darlene Miller with the Decorah eagles, James Deal, Amanda Nicholson with the Wildlife Center of Virginia, Hope Rutledge, Lori Naumann and the Minnesota DNR Nongame Wildlife Program, Bill Route and Jim Campbell-Spickler with the National Park Service's eaglet survey, Rachel Bauer, and Wildwoods Rehabilitation Center of Duluth.

Photo Credits by Photographer and Page Number

Front cover: James R. Deal (eagle release); Shutterstock (eagle close-up)

Back cover: James R. Deal (held eagle); Glenn E. Miller (flying eagle); University of Minnesota, The Raptor Center: (exam)

Rachel Bauer: 30 (nest); Jim Campbell-Spickler: 30 (growing, fish); James R. Deal: 12, 25, 29, 31 (flight); Peter Gove: 32; L. Darlene Miller: 8 (falling birds 1 and 4), 11, 27; Glenn E. Miller: 8 (falling birds 2 and 3), 10, 22, 28; Minnesota Department of Natural Resources, Nongame Wildlife Program: 30 (eggs, hatch); University of Minnesota, The Raptor Center: 14 (both), 15 (both), 16, 17, 18, 21, 30 (claws), 31 (juvenile, mature); Bill Route with the National Park Service: 4 (both), 8 (tree), 23; Hope Rutledge: 5, 7, 26; Wildwoods: 13

Edited by Ryan Jacobson

Cover and book design by Jonathan Norberg

10 9 8 7 6 5 4 3 2 1
Copyright 2015 by Christie Gove-Berg
Published by Adventure Publications, Inc.
820 Cleveland Street South
Cambridge, MN 55008
1-800-678-7006
www.adventurepublications.net
Printed in China
ISBN: 978-1-59193-542-1

Esther the Eaglet

A True Story of Rescue and Rehabilitation

Esther is a three-month-old eaglet. She nests with her parents near the top of a tall pine tree. Her favorite food is fish. Her favorite season is spring. Her favorite weather is wind.

In fact, wind is one of Esther's favorite things of all, especially when it blows through her new flight feathers. Her mother and father warn her to be careful, but Esther just wants to fly.

One gray day, while Esther's parents are out hunting, a strong wind begins to blow. The wind pushes the branches of Esther's pine tree and moves her nest back and forth, back and forth.

The rocking nest makes Esther curious. She lifts her wings, and the wind tickles her feathers. It feels good.

Esther stretches her wings higher and higher. Suddenly, she is lifted up! She tries to pull her wings down, but the wind holds them open.

She tumbles sideways. She is lifted up again like a kite. Then the wind softens, and Esther drops down, down, down . . .

CRASH!

Esther lands on the forest floor in a heap. She stands and tries to raise her wings again, but she lets out a shrill whistle. In her left wing there is a new sensation: pain.

She looks around and notices people in the distance. They are watching her. She whistles in fear.

A car arrives and a woman gets out. She is trained and knows what to do. She sneaks slowly toward Esther.

In a sudden, surprising motion, the woman scoops up Esther and puts her in a small, dark place. Now Esther can only hear the growl of the car engine and the beat of her heart.

When Esther is taken out of the dark box, she is in a different place, called a Raptor Center. It is like a hospital for eagles and other raptors. The room is full of strange equipment.

Esther is achy, angry and afraid. People move carefully and quietly around her. One of them gently places her on a tall table. With her sharp eyes, Esther watches the people closely.

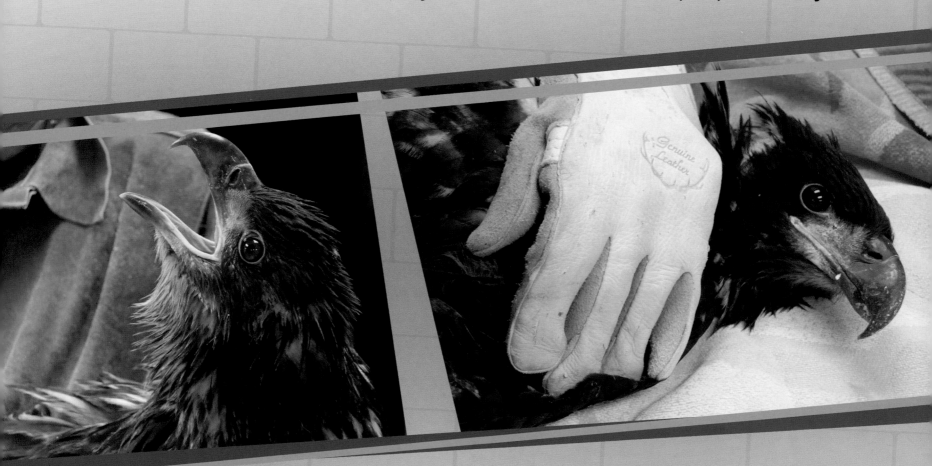

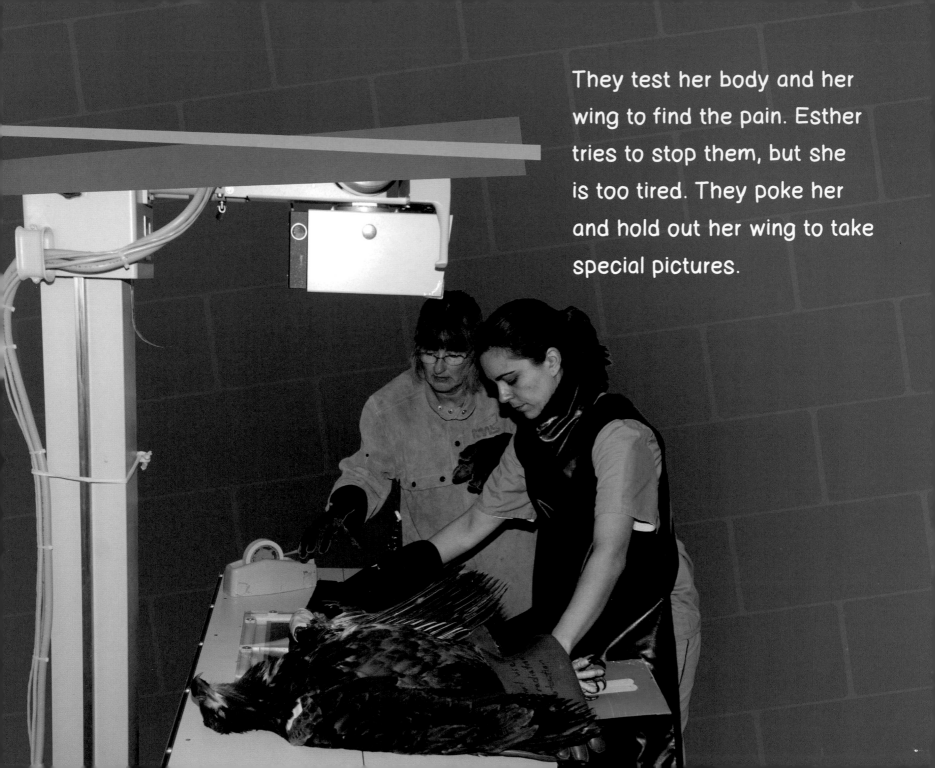

They test her body and her wing to find the pain. Esther tries to stop them, but she is too tired. They poke her and hold out her wing to take special pictures.

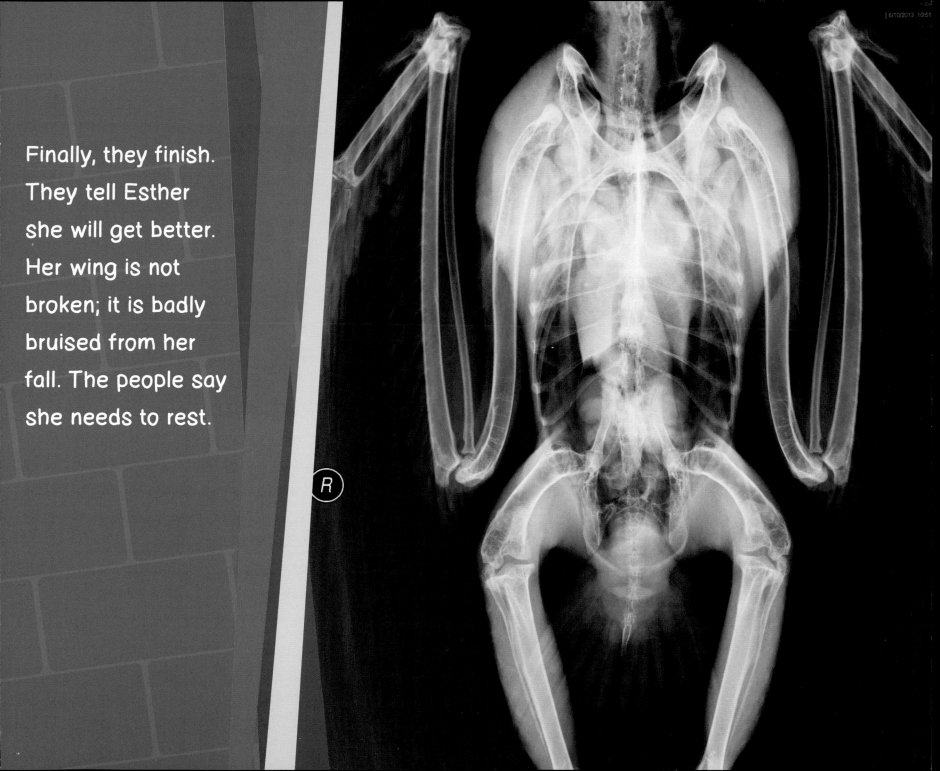

Finally, they finish. They tell Esther she will get better. Her wing is not broken; it is badly bruised from her fall. The people say she needs to rest.

That night, they leave Esther alone in a box. There is fish to eat, but Esther is not hungry. Her box has a window, and she looks out into the darkness. Other birds are there, too, and their sounds echo around her.

Esther misses her mother and father. She wishes, more than anything, to be home with them again.

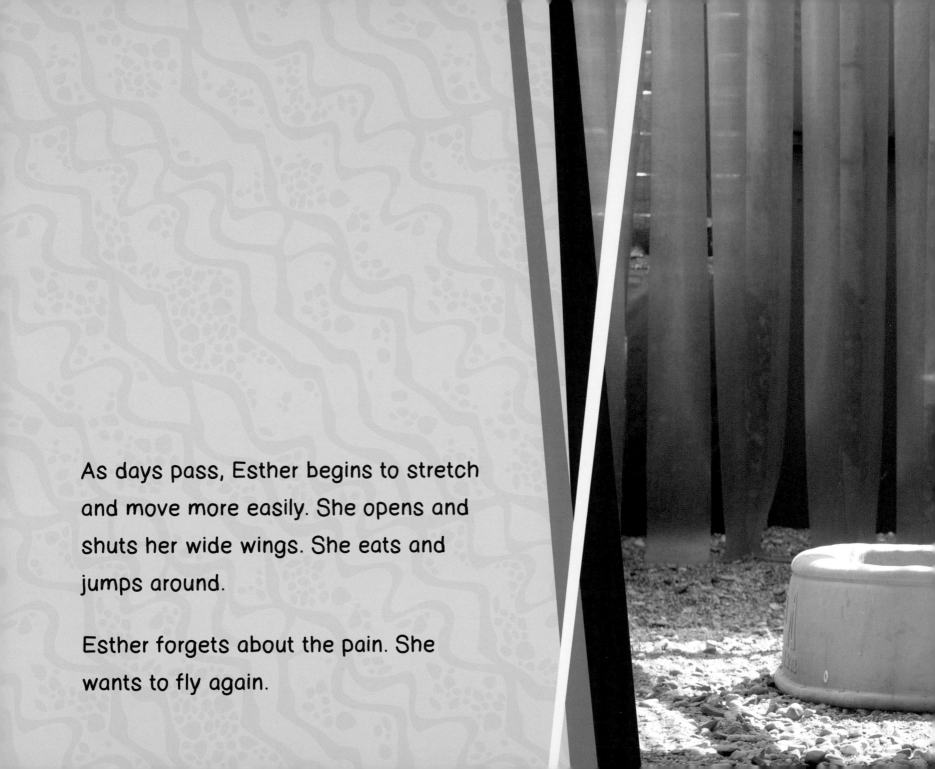

As days pass, Esther begins to stretch and move more easily. She opens and shuts her wide wings. She eats and jumps around.

Esther forgets about the pain. She wants to fly again.

The people take her to a large field. They place a band around her ankles.

Esther flaps her wings and lifts off the ground. She feels wind below her. She is flying! Mother and Father would be so proud.

The ankle bands tug at her feet. They keep Esther from flying away. She must land again. She whistles in anger.

The next day, Esther stays in the dark box. The box is loaded into a loud car, and the car drives away. Where are the people taking Esther? Her heart races.

When Esther comes out of the box, she recognizes her parents' territory. She is almost home!

Many new people have gathered. They are quiet and their eyes are kind. Esther winks her eye at the smallest one, and he claps his hands and calls out, "I hope she flies! I hope she flies!"

Esther opens her wings, and the people gasp. Esther knows just what to do.

Flapping her strong wings, she flies up to perch on a tree branch and calls to her mother and father. The people wave and cheer for her.

Esther hears her father's familiar whistle. She sees her mother circling in the blue sky above. Esther opens her strong wings and flies to her nest.

Closing her eyes, she feels the wind in her feathers. She is just in time to eat fresh fish that her parents have caught for her.

Esther is home, and she is healthy. She has been rescued and rehabilitated. She is happy to be returned to the wild.

And she still loves the wind.

Tell me more about Esther's journey.

After Esther fell, she was found hopping along the forest floor in Osceola, Wisconsin, near the Saint Croix River. The people who found her called The Raptor Center at the University of Minnesota. A volunteer came and brought Esther to the Raptor Center. Veterinarians tested her for infection, lead poisoning and broken bones. Her wing was bruised from the fall, but it was not broken. Esther stayed at the Raptor Center for a few days, while her wing healed. She was released in the same area where she was found, and she returned to the nest with her parents.

Does a baby Bald Eagle look like an adult Bald Eagle?

No, an eaglet is dark brown with white spots on its body. It has a brown beak and eyes. Every year, an eagle molts (loses and regrows) its feathers. At five years old, a Bald Eagle's head and tail are white; its beak and eyes turn yellow.

How do eaglets learn to fly?

Eaglets begin to fly when they are about three months old. They start by stretching and jumping in the nest and on branches around the nest. This is called branching. As they hop around the nest tree, they get stronger. At some point, they are strong enough to take off and fly. This is called fledging. An eaglet's flight feathers are larger than an adult's feathers, which makes it easier to learn how to fly. Believe it or not, learning to land is even harder than learning to fly.

What are eagle nests like?

Bald Eagles build large stick nests. The nests can be about six feet across and six feet tall and can weigh as much as a car. Nests are built at the top of large trees—usually near water, such as a river or lake. The mom lays up to three eggs. Both the mom and dad help to incubate the eggs (keep them warm), and both parents help to feed and care for the eaglets after they hatch.

What do Bald Eagles eat?

A Bald Eagle's favorite food is fish, but eagles also eat carrion (dead animals) and small prey, such as birds, turtles and rabbits.

What is a raptor center?

A raptor center is a place that studies raptors, cares for injured birds and teaches people about them. A raptor is a meat-eating bird, like a Bald Eagle. All raptors share three characteristics: excellent eyesight, sharp talons and a hooked beak. There are 482 species of raptors in the world.

build the nest   lay the eggs   eggs hatch in 30 days   growing up

How do injured birds get to raptor centers?

When people see injured raptors, they should call a raptor center for help. Sometimes the raptor center will explain how to pick up the bird and bring it safely to the raptor center. Other times a volunteer will go to the injured bird and bring it to the raptor center.

What do raptor centers do for injured birds?

Raptor centers care for any and all injuries that occur to raptors. The most common injuries are broken bones, bruised bones, infection and lead poisoning. Often, the raptor center is able to treat the raptor and return it to the wild, but sometimes the raptor is too injured to be saved. Once in a while, a raptor is treated and saved but cannot be returned to the wild. In those cases, the bird is trained for use in education programs.

Why are some eagles getting treated for lead poisoning?

Hunters who use lead shot in their guns accidentally leave lead shot in the remains of dead animals. Eagles eat those dead animals and end up eating the lead, too. It only takes a small amount of lead to kill an eagle. Hunters can help to prevent lead poisoning by choosing non-lead ammunition for their guns.

How does a raptor center know when a bird can return home?

The bird needs to be able to fly and to feed itself before it can be released into the wild. Just like human athletes need to practice to get better, birds need to practice flying. Thin leather straps, called jesses (JESS-ez), are attached to each leg of the bird. The jesses are connected to a long line called a creance (KREE-ents). Volunteers exercise the bird in a large field several times per week until the bird is ready for release.

first flight at 3 months

becoming adult: 4–5 years

mature adult: 5–7 years

Does it cost a lot of money to take care of all those birds?

Yes, it does. Much of the funding comes from public donations, so if you like Esther's story, consider supporting your local raptor center. By buying this book, you are supporting The Raptor Center at the University of Minnesota, which cares for eagles, hawks, owls, vultures, osprey and falcons.

Tell me more about The Raptor Center at the University of Minnesota.

The Raptor Center is part of the University of Minnesota College of Veterinary Medicine. Each year, the Raptor Center cares for more than 900 sick and injured raptors, while also supporting ongoing raptor research. The Raptor Center helps to train veterinary students and veterinarians from around the world in raptor medicine and conservation. The Raptor Center also puts on public education programs and special events, so people can learn more about raptors.

Can I watch Bald Eagles, even if none live nearby?

Absolutely! If you want to watch an eagle family in action, search online for an eagle webcam. An eagle webcam is a camera placed above a live eagle nest. People can watch on their computers as the eagles raise and care for their young.

About the Author

Christie Gove-Berg writes fiction and poetry, but the rescue of an injured eaglet on her parents' land moved her to write *Esther the Eaglet*, a nonfiction tale of an eaglet's journey. To accurately portray Esther's story, Christie worked closely with The Raptor Center at the University of Minnesota, an experience both educational and inspiring. A portion of the profits for each book will go to the Raptor Center. This is Christie's first children's book.

Her other published work includes "The Delivery," an essay in the November 2009 issue of *Minnesota Medicine*, and "Proof," a poem in *Talking Stick*, Volume 23, Fall 2014.

Christie has been a member of the Forest Lake Writer's Workshop for seven years. She spends her days treating patients as a family medicine physician, and she spends her free time with her family.